Revelations from a

Black Girl *Bloomin'*

Chandra Meadows

Cover Illustration by Kamon Ross

Printed in the United States of America

First Printing, 2017

ISBN-13:9780692900888

ISBN-10: 0692900888

Black Evolution Media and Publishing Company
www.blackevolutionmedia.com

DEDICATION

To freedom.
To self-awareness.
To growth.
To blossoming.

CONTENTS

When a black girl blooms, she becomes.
Here's to becoming...

What it means to "Bloom"...

Bloom is a term often associated with flowers. To bloom means to open up, to grow and develop. Blooming is the process of allowing yourself to go through changes in order to meet a higher version of who you are.

Black girls and women in particular, tend to have a hard time flourishing freely. So often we are given labels and placed in boxes that do not leave much room for us to grow. These conditions are not favorable for our progression. In order for one to completely bloom, the environment must be properly cultivated. Certain seeds must be planted, the soil must be watered, and sunlight must be present.

If I had a diary, and you opened it up, these pages would fall out. Revelations from a Black Girl Bloomin' is a declaration of freedom. It's me taking back the power I had let escape me long ago. After all the mistakes I've made and the lessons I've learned, blooming into who I am today was inevitable. Within this book you may see reflections of yourself or even women you know, or have known.

This is an ode to black girls and women who are glowing up, blossoming, flourishing, finding beauty in their truth, and unapologetically bloomin' on their own terms.

The chapters are broken down into phases similar to the life cycle of a flower. I begin the book with seeds that were initially planted within my soul (soil), then I move on to how I found the silver lining(sunlight) in the circumstances and experiences I've had while on my journey, which eventually birthed the truths I was able to water in order to bloom into a new awareness of self. Blooming never ends. As long as you are constantly evolving, and feeding the parts of you that connect to your highest self, you will always be in a state of bloom.

Welcome to Revelations from a Black Girl Bloomin'...

SEEDS.

(the seeds planted in my consciousness
to produce my initial reality)

/The Beginning.

Initially, adapting to this world was a journey in itself.
According to my mother,
I had random seizures as a baby.
I died in my grandmother's arms once and came back.
The doctors told my mother I would be
a little "slower" than other kids.
I don't think anyone ever found out exactly
why I was having these seizures in the first place.
Well, the "why" was never told to me anyway.
Maybe coming into this world shocked my system,
Or maybe I was simply trying to do my own
variation of the Harlem shake?
Either way, the doctors were wrong.
I wasn't "slower". I was right on time.
Perhaps even a little ahead.

/Childhood.

I was always a curious child.
The world and its inhabitants always intrigued me.
Science and history were subjects I connected with early in life.
I was bursting with creative energy,
which led to a whole lot of self-expression.
Most times, the ways I expressed myself were not received well.
You see, my expression came in forms of exploring truths,
questioning the status quo,
and the need to know the "why" to everything.
I often daydream about the kind of child I used to be.
Before I was silenced.
Before I knew the taste of rejection.
Before my little bubble was burst.
Before I discovered not everyone wanted to be free,
how hard it was for most of us to face ourselves,
and how easy it is to lose who we are within a system
we were taught to accept as customary.
I started to lose the spark I came into the world with,
as many of us do.
I didn't realize what was happening
until I reached the humbling stages of adulthood.

/Childhood Blues.

The seeds that were planted
in the soil of my childhood,
were seeds of lack.
Opportunities were limited.
Money was scarce.
My father nonexistent.
Self-esteem was never properly cultivated.
I only knew "not enough".
I was most familiar with feelings
of not being good enough,
not being pretty enough,
not being rich enough,
just not being enough,
and this affected my whole outlook on life.
Most importantly, It affected my view of myself.
As a young girl, I had already discovered how unfair life could be.
Why couldn't I have what everyone else had?
I was convinced that everyone was a part of this exclusive "club"
that allowed them to live these good, healthy, normal lifestyles, I
wasn't privileged to. I didn't even get both feet grounded into
the earth, before I gave up on thinking I could ever experience
the gift of true happiness.

/Mother Dearest.

I wonder if my mother ever found out
Who she was before me?
I mean how much
can a little girl know
about herself at 16?

/Abuse.

Seeing a parent abused can snatch the innocence away from a child. The first time I heard my mom getting beaten, was the first time I truly felt helplessness and hate. I didn't fully understand what was happening, but I knew it was nothing good. After hearing what sounded like thunder knocking up against thick skin, a light appeared from the darkest corner of the room I shared with my brother and sister. It was my mom coming in to check on us, or maybe she was coming in to see if we had heard the boxing match? She saw that I was awake. She knew that I knew. We never talked about that night and I never forgot it.
That night changed me.
I didn't know it then, but it did.
I was never the same after.

/Abuse Part II.

The abuse continued for years.
It became more than physical.
It was emotional.
It was mental.
It was spiritual warfare.
All symptoms of a love affair gone rogue.
Bearing witness to it was damaging to my innocence, but it was also one of my first encounters with the reality of things not always being "good".
I learned that "bad" existed too.

/Dysfunction.

People make homes out of dysfunction.
I suppose you make due
the best way you can
with what you are given.

/Motherly Love.

I love my mother with everything in me
but I don't think we ever connected
as mother and daughter.
I always felt there was something stopping her from
fully coming into motherhood.
From fully loving.
From fully being free.
From fully standing in her own truth.
Maybe she just never learned how.
What's more tragic,
the child in need of love,
or the mother?

/Fatherless Daughter.

You are automatically diagnosed
with all of these character flaws
when you don't have a daddy.
Fatherless daughters get a bad rap.
You quickly become the girl with "daddy issues".
Growing up without a father leaves you in pieces
and society has a way of magnifying this.
You always feel like there's a piece of you missing.
Like there's this big hole that you just can't seem to fill, no matter
what you try to fill it with. Nothing works. The hole remains.
Some spend their entire lives trying to fill this void.
Never knowing what it's like to have your daddy kiss
you on the forehead.
Never knowing what it feels like to hear your daddy tell
you how much he loves you, and how beautiful you are.
Not knowing how to connect with the masculine energy
you were deprived of.
It's painful.
Being labeled defective because you were
denied something you had no control over
is soul crushing.
Not having a father around solidified
my feelings of not being enough.
But I didn't want to be like those girls,
you know, the ones deemed broken by society.
So I pretended I wasn't.
I pretended so well, I no longer recognized myself.

/Esteem.

I think people can smell
when you doubt the love you have for yourself.
Having low self-esteem is like wearing cheap perfume.
It reeks.
And once some people pick up on that scent,
you become an easy prey.
People can be cruel,
especially kids,
but they are only recycling what they were taught.
I didn't feel ugly until I was treated as if I were.

/Other Girls.

I envied girls who were told they were beautiful,
and actually believed it.
Who did they think they were?
How dare they prance around with their heads high,
and speak as if they had the world
in the palm of their hands?
They were everything I wanted to be,
but had no idea how to be it.
Where do you learn to think highly of yourself?
I admired the girls who were able to be girls.
The girls who seemed to move
gracefully through life,
as everyone bowed in awe.
I wanted to be like those girls,
yet...
I found myself being the girl
standing in the back
on the sidelines,
wishing for whatever magic
they seemed to possess.
I had no idea that I had it too.

/Black Features.

I was a black child with dark skin,
thick hair, a big nose, and full lips.
I was a target.
The way I looked represented
everything we were taught to hate.
What becomes of the young girl (or boy),
who's told their skin is too dark, and their lips too big?
It was the words of others that changed what I saw in my mirror.
Forget the fact that I was one of the smartest in the room,
nor did it matter that I was a nice girl.
I wore the mark that oppressed my ancestors.
The mark that produced hate in the hearts of those without it.
The mark that created separation between those
whose features weren't as "black".
My skin was dark, hair nappy, nose big, and lips full.
This was my "scarlet letter".
I questioned God often during this time of my life.
Why did he have to make my skin so black,
and hair so nappy?
He never answered me back then,
or perhaps I just wasn't ready to listen.

/The Misadventures of Black Hair.

A black girl and her hair can be the best of friends,
or the worst of enemies.
My hair and I were arch nemesis.
I was not taught how to love her.
I was not taught what to feed her.
I was not taught how to manage her.
So I covered her.
I covered her with layers of hair
that did not belong to me.
I hid her roots out of embarrassment.
She was not acceptable to the world.
So I hid her and all her glory.
But I was not just hiding hair,
I was hiding a part of me.
In my eyes, that was just the price I had to pay.
It was better than facing my nappy roots.
Although it made me even more self-conscious,
I wore hair weaves for years,
and when I wasn't wearing weaves,
I was getting my hair strung out on the creamy crack.
I was taught to be ashamed of the hair that grew from my scalp.
It did not look like the hair models
on the hair products advertised to me,
so I bought hair that was.

Chandra Meadows

/Misrepresentation.

The lack of black representation within society has a penetrating
psychological effect on the black community.
We are taught we are the minority.
We are taught that we can't fit
within this society without
shedding shades of our blackness.
It becomes an issue the moment black Americans
find pride in black culture,
yet we are supposed to be proud Americans?
As if America hasn't been responsible for
repeatedly stripping away our humanity.
While black culture has always been popular,
black people, not so much.
Those outside of the black community,
still haven't figured out that it's the people
that make the culture, not the other way around.
Today, we are probably experiencing the most
inauthentic surge of black representation.
The black experience is trendy.
It makes for good headlines.
But black people are still being
mistreated,
murdered,
and turned into hashtags.

/Feminism.

Is there space for the black woman
within the feminist movement?
I've noticed the conflict that comes
when a black woman must choose
between her blackness and her womanhood.
This is a conflict exclusive to the black woman.
You have to fight for your right as a woman on this day,
and your right to be black the next.
It's tiring.
It's hard for me to solely focus on my rights as a woman,
while my rights to be black are being stepped on,
and it's equally hard to throw up my fist for my blackness,
when my womanhood is being threatened.
So where does this leave me?
Where does this leave any woman
who has to fight for her right to just be present
as a black woman?

/Black Men.

I do not see black men as my enemy,
but it's been an internal struggle trying to digest the pain caused
by the men I've encountered throughout my life.
Still, I will not turn my back on my brothers,
even though the burden of hurt and disappointment
weighs heavy upon my back,
as if I am paying for the sins of my father's absence.
I will fight for you because I see the purpose
in your crown and I understand
that we share Godly reflections.

/Suicidal Thoughts.

Suicide can be a hard thing to discuss in the black community. Telling someone you don't want to be anymore, is probably the most awkward conversation one can have. It's something no one is ever truly prepared for. So most of the time, it's a conversation that is never had. How do you explain that you want to release yourself from yourself, even if it meant taking your own life?
Thoughts of suicide can be tricky.
It plays on your weaknesses.
It feeds on your insecurities.
It gets off on your fears.
Thoughts of suicide came to me at different stages of my life. It usually showed up during the times when I found it most difficult to deal with myself and my circumstances.
Thoughts associated with suicide will have you feeling like you have absolutely nothing to live for,
or like there's no reason for you to be here (alive).
You don't see that the very fact that you are here (alive),
is proof that you should be (alive).
The thoughts aren't rooted in logic.
It's all emotionally driven.
It's an escape and a dramatic cry for help
and there were times when I nearly
drowned in my own tears.
Thank God I learned to swim.

/Desperation.

The first guy to ever break up with me, was also the first guy I ever gave my heart to. I mean I had no idea I could even feel what I felt for this man. The feeling was so potent, it drove me mad. I made myself belief he was "the one" for me. I tried to make him believe it too. When he decided to break up with me the first time, it wasn't so bad. It was the second time that came like a stab into the deepest part of my heart. You know that saying "never let someone tell you they don't want you twice"? Well, I was told and shown more times than I can count.
You would think that would've made me walk away right?
If I was being logical and not blinded by infatuation,
I would have.
If I was not drunk off the possibility of this man being my forever,
I would have.
Even if I had loved myself just a little bit more,
I would have.
But I didn't,
at least not right away.
I continued to give my heart, mind, and body to a man that made it known on countless occasions that he did not want me. I was attached to the idea of him I had formed in my mind, and I was foolish enough to think I could change his mind to fit mine. So I put up with being treated like I wasn't good enough.
I was searching for my value
within a man who knew I lacked self-worth.
"Why do you let me treat you like this?",
he asked me one day.
"Because you don't care about yourself, that's why".
His words haunted me for months…

/After The Fall.

I was thirsty for more of the love that had awakened within me.
I thought he was the ocean that was going to supply
the water I needed to rid my soul of this thirst.
But I just ended up high and dry.
It took me a while to realize that
I was the ocean I needed to drink from.

/My Mother's Reflection.

We hardly ever think we favor our mothers, even if we are constantly told, "You look just like your mother, child".
As you politely smile and wonder if you really do favor her.
My mother and I share many features.
She's a beautiful woman.
High cheek bones,
Full lips,
Smooth dark brown skin.
People would often tell me
how much they thought we looked alike,
some even called us twins.
But the day I saw my mother's reflection in my own,
did not come from a random glance into the bathroom mirror,
it came from an experience.
The night an ex-boyfriend decided to put his arm around my neck
in the attempt to feed the ego of his own demons,
was the day my mother's face became my own.
It was then I realized I was in the midst of continuing a cycle that
had plagued the women in my family for generations.
It was then I realized I did not want to share that same reflection.

/Ex-Lessons.

I can identify certain issues I had within myself
based off who I was attracting at different stages of my life.
Each man represented a part of me
I needed to either change,
or be made more aware of.
If you pay attention to the type of lovers that appear in your life,
you will be able to see the lessons you need to learn from them.
I will never regret any of the interactions I've had with the men
I have dated, because at one point,
I needed them just as much as they needed me.
We are all here to grow and change each other
with every interaction, encounter, and experience.
Sometimes it's pleasurable and sometimes it stings.
 Everyone is not meant to be your forever,
but that doesn't mean they won't change you forever.

/Changes.

Change was something I was forced to get used to
early in life. We moved around a lot when I was a kid.
From house to house, school to school,
change became a thing I despised.
It brought on anxiety.
It made me feel unstable.
It was hard seeing the beauty of change back then.
Change only brought me discomfort,
disconnection, and the longing to know
how it felt to just stand still.

/Let's Talk About Sex Baby.

Talks of sexuality is yet another thing that barely makes it to a black family's dinner table. I had to learn about sex and sexuality through trial and error. I lost my virginity at 23.
It had nothing to do with love, I had love for my partner but I wasn't in love with him. He had provided the comfort of friendship. Originally, I had these lavish plans to save myself for marriage. I was taught by way of religion that it was the "right" thing to do. Curiosity ended up winning in the end.
I went ahead and got the physical act of sex out of the way.
But the emotional and spiritual sides of it,
were much harder to obtain and understand.
Everyone you lay down with,
you connect with in some way.
Their energy locks unto yours and vice versa.
We have all heard the saying,
"You are what you eat",
well you are who you sleep with.
Pay attention to how you
feel,
act,
and think,
after you've let someone enter your temple.
You are not just laying down with a body,
you are laying down with their energy and spirit,
their angels and their demons,
their beliefs, their fears,
and their partners before you,
and you are getting back up with traces of their soul
entangled within the web of your own.

/Sexual Libations.

Sexuality is often awkwardly expressed in this culture.
Boys learn one thing and girls seem to learn another.
Where boys may be glorified.
Girls are shamed.
Where girls may be taught sacredness.
Boys are taught something more profane.
And then we are expected to meet somewhere in the middle of it
all to somehow find mutual love, truth, and understanding.

/Remembering The Time.

I remember when I kissed the son of the owner
of the after school program I was attending.
Another boy, slightly older, caught us.
He told me if I didn't let him touch on me,
he would tell on us.
I was horrified.
If I hesitated or said no,
he would sing Michael Jackson's *Remember The Time*.
This happened each time he wanted to touch me.
I never heard that song the same after that.
In fact, I stopped hearing the song completely.
To this day, each time the song plays,
my mind goes right back to my 10 or 11-year-old self
being too afraid to tell a boy NO.

/The Set-Up.

Being violated by someone you considered family,
is such a peculiar devastation. You think about every interaction
and every conversation you've had with that person. Was it all a
ploy to get to that very moment they decided to put you in a
compromising position? Was it all a part of some masterplan to
take away a piece of your soul in order to appease their own?
The day the man I considered family violated me,
was the day I grew wings and flew away.
But he still dwells in the space I once called home,
as if it never happened.
But I can't seem to forget it.
Sometimes it's even replayed in my thoughts
as I search for the "why".
Why did he think it was okay?
Why did I not see it coming?
Why do my family continue to move
as if it never happened?

/Keeping It All In The Family.

Why do black families have so many damn secrets?
Everyone's closet is filled with these skeletons
they try so hard to keep hidden
from their children and their children's children.
Does it ever cross their minds that
keeping those skeletons in their homes
may be the cause of certain generational curses
continuing to flow through their bloodlines?
Do they ever consider that by sharing these experiences
they may actually heal the parts of themselves
that may be holding on to the pain?
Or possibly even saving a loved one
from having to endure the same unfortunate fate?
Learning some of my family's secrets
shattered the glass bubble I was living in.
It was painfully uncomfortable
but it freed me.

/Witches.

I believe the women in my family
were witches in a past life.
Not the eerie depiction of witches you see conjured up by
Hollywood, but real life sorcerers.
They have such a distinct power about them.
The things they have been through,
The common story lines they share,
The things they keep hidden within their closet of skeletons.
I often look at them in awe.
Amazed at how they seem to have mastered resilience.
I am proud to be connected to this type of strength.
But I am also aware that there's a lot of
darkness that dwells in its presence.
Negative forces have blocked
generational blessings and replaced them
with the curse of discontentment,
silence and struggle.
Maybe this is the ancestors way
of slapping them in the face
in the attempt to wake them up?
Hoping that they see they are more than able
to reclaim the powers they were given,
and how they possess the magic to heal themselves.

/What About Your Friends?

I've always had friends,
even when I didn't put in much effort to make them.
I've had a set of friends for every phase of my life.
I've formed bonds and created memories
with people whose energy drew to mine
during whichever season.
And I've suffered from a broken heart
each time our paths parted ways for whatever reason.
I am still in search of friendships that do not crash
whenever there's turbulence.
Friendships that flourish in the presence of growth,
Friendships that can stand the test of time.
A tribe of those who are in constant transformation.
A tribe that welcomes wanderers with open arms.

/Poor.

There are levels to being poor.
What you consider poor may be
luxurious living to someone else,
and what you consider luxury,
could be the bottom of the barrel to another.
For me, poor has always been a mindset
but I have been reminded
during different times of my life
how "poor" can manifest itself in the physical.

/Lack.

When you are used to being without,
you will continue to put out energy
that attracts more of nothingness.
When you come from a poor, religious, black family,
somewhere along the way you are indirectly taught
these ignorant hang-ups about money and wealth.
You are taught how to live pay check to pay check,
you are taught that at the root of money lies evil,
you are taught that it is something
you will always have to chase.
So you spend your life in constant pursuit of it,
or you accept that you will never have enough.

Chandra Meadows

/The Intimidation of Success.

Success has always been the goal,
but it also gives me a slight case of anxiety.
With success comes more accountability.
With success comes more responsibility.
With success comes trying to always live up
to that first successful high.
I mean I can take failure all day,
we have had our rounds in the ring,
but success,
that can be terrifying.
It's intimidating.
How do you fail gracefully after meeting success once?
"It is our light not our darkness that most frightens us",
this line has always stood out to me.
Most of us are not running from darkness,
yet it is in darkness,
we are hiding from our own light.

/Miseducation.

I love to feed my mind new things.
School was something I valued.
I believe learning is something
that should be continuous.
I was in the gifted program.
I made the honor's list.
I had the experience of college.
But over time, my feelings about school started to change.
I realized it was more of a training camp
to "civilize" and regurgitate.
Of course it's all what you make it
but I no longer believed
institutionalized education
was the only way to be successful.
Dropping out of college wasn't intentional
but my passion for it had died.
I went into a state of depression afterwards.
I wasn't supposed to be the "College Dropout".
But here I am.

/The Internship.

I interned at a law firm once.
The internship itself wasn't much of a learning experience.
I ended up being let go.
Yes, I was fired from an internship.
The administrative assistant
who I was to answer to
seemed to have something against me.
She didn't attempt to teach me anything.
Every time I would ask a question about
how something was supposed to go or be,
She would simply say "Google it".
It was then I realized,
no one was going to give me the game.
No one was going to hold my hand to success
and no one owed me anything.
If I wanted it,
I was going to have to go out and get it.

WATER + SUNLIGHT.

(finding the silver lining in circumstances and experiences,
and watering the truths that birthed from them)

You would have thought the seeds planted within me would have sprouted weeds,

But au contraire.

/More Changes.

We will go through a million changes
and have a million experiences
before really understanding who we are,
and even then,
there will be even more changes
and experiences just around the corner.
If you are living,
you are constantly growing
and constantly changing.
Changes are reminders that you are alive.

/Bad Seeds.

The seeds that were planted within my consciousness early on,
were not the seeds I wanted to continue to feed and water.
I started to see how problematic
some of my thoughts and beliefs were.
If I wanted to grow into my highest self,
I had to release the parts of me
that didn't align with the person I wanted to become.
It's okay to dig up the seeds
that are not favorable to your growth.
You have to make room for new seeds.
Seeds that will build you up,
not break you down.
Seeds that will absorb your water
and transcend in your sunlight.

/The Stories We tell.

I started to erase the stories
I had embedded in my mind
that were not true to who I was.
I had to dig a little deeper to get to thoughts of abundance.
The thoughts of lack I had been housing
were only attracting more deficiency.
Everything starts as a mindset.
If you think you are less than,
that is what you will be.
If you think you lack something,
you will attract things and people
who will magnify whatever it is you think you lack.
If you think you are not good enough,
you won't be.
The stories we tell ourselves and the thoughts we think,
are the co-creators for the lives we lead.
Once I started changing my story,
my thoughts started to evolve,
and once my thoughts started to evolve,
my life started to unfold in the most beautiful way.

/Stay Woke.

When you sleep on yourself because of fear,
or out of doubt,
the universe will see to it
that you never find comfort in settling.
You will find misery in every space you try to hide in.
It will taunt you until you wake up
and become everything you were created to be.

/Self-Love.

We must be everything to ourselves
before we can ever be anything to anyone else.
If people found love within themselves
and fell utterly in love with what they found,
there would be less dependency
on obtaining love from outside of ourselves.
Placing so much pressure on others,
demanding that they love us,
when we haven't even discovered
how to truly love ourselves,
is a selfish act.
Ironically,
self-love births selflessness.

/Anxiousness.

Is anxiety a result of a fear and self-doubt concoction?
And if you actually believe in God, or a divine higher power, why
do you even allow this doubt to consume you? What do you
have to be afraid of? Are you not fully committed to your belief?
These are some of the questions I asked myself.
I have suffered from anxiety for some time now.
I've spent the last few years working to find it's root,
but I've discovered,
you don't take away years of built up anxiety all at once.
You have to cut it out,
little by little,
and before you know it,
you are free.

/Crown.

We will all be forced to reposition our crowns
during various moments of our journey,
no one ever said carrying a crown was easy.
So when you feel the weight of your crown
becoming a little too much to bear,
just breathe,
readjust,
and find your groove again.

/Bye Bye Doubt.

Self-doubt is the beginning of your own destruction,
But belief in yourself
will take you right into the depths
of endless possibilities.

/Space.

It's amazing how much the universe
will open up to you
once you stop thinking
it is against you.

/The Balancing Act.

Life is all about balance.
Just as we embrace the good things that happen to us,
we must also embrace what we perceive as bad.
Of course embracing the bad will be harder,
but usually, we learn the most during our most trying times.
Understanding the balance of good and bad
will allow you to see the greater picture.
If you only prepare for the good things
and react irrationally when things happen
that may not be as good,
you will constantly end up at mental roadblocks
and emotional dead ends.
Unfortunately, we aren't properly taught balance.
We are told that happiness should be the goal,
but never taught how to handle pain.
We are taught to do good,
but never taught how to deal with the bad we do.
Realizing that you cannot have a positive without its negative,
will create a blissful balance in your life.
You will be able to see things as whole
instead of in fragments.
Finding balance will have you out here
smiling more and worrying less because
once you find your balance,
it decreases the possibility of a fall.

/The Savior Complex.

We wait for our lives to get better,
or for someone to come save us,
not realizing that we are the only ones
with the true capability to save ourselves.
Saving yourself will require you to be honest with yourself,
and it involves a whole lot of inner work.
Everyone's not up for the challenge.
Many avoid taking accountability over their own lives.
So instead of saving themselves, they wait.
They wait for a savior to come,
unaware that the savior has always been within.

/Psychological Resilience.

Life comes bearing many gifts.
One gift in particular life has given me,
is the gift of resiliency.
Within this system that seem to be designed to break us,
resilience will often be your lifeline.

/One helluva Ride.

In life,
there's always a series of twists and turns
and peaks and valleys.
We won't always get it right but
we won't always get it wrong either.
Life is a journey that is supposed to change
and mold us along the way.
It is filled with mistake making,
lesson learning,
heartbreaking,
celebrating,
starting over,
dead ends,
new beginnings,
breathtaking,
rerouting,
past reflecting,
future predicting,
present living,
soul searching,
love chasing,
elevating,
evolving,
forever changing moments.
So you might as well enjoy the ride.

/The Inferiority Myth.

We are taught inferiority the moment we open up a history book.
People who look like me were
chained,
shackled,
and whipped in this country.
This was the first thing I learned about my history.
Think about what that does to a child.
Depression and low self-esteem plague
the hoods and inner cities the most.
Hope is taken away from us before we ever
understand what hope is,
or sometimes our hope is found within
the pages of a book that is supposed
to bring us some sort of salvation.
Some of us are lucky,
and escape that mentality
of not feeling like we matter,
or those detrimental thoughts of never having,
or being enough.
And once we rid ourselves of this plague,
we begin to see new light.
We establish new faith.
We learn to celebrate our blackness.
Black power becomes our truth,
not out of hate but out of necessity, out of virtue.
We start to believe in ourselves
after being taught the complete opposite.
No, there are no apologies for seeing the beauty in my own
genetic makeup, nor will I feel sorry for celebrating my culture,
and embracing those who share the same origins as me.
This is about taking back the pages
that were stolen from our story.
This is about reclaiming my space in a world
that tried so hard to convince me I didn't belong.
This is about redemption.

/Equality.

We spend a lot of time trying
to convince people
we are equal to them.
Time that would be better spent
convincing ourselves
that we don't need their permission or approval.

/Be Humble.

We are taught to be humble,
which usually leads to many people
downplaying themselves
in order to make others comfortable,
and more accepting of their presence.
What's wrong with believing in ourselves?
What's wrong with being proud of who we are
and wanting to express that?
Why is it so unbecoming to fully move in our light and truth?
We are all one of one.
Don't belittle yourself fearing the judgements
of those who are intimidated by the power you possess.
We were put here to unlock our fullest potential.
We were put here to be great in our own right.
Misguided attributes of humbleness
will have you underappreciated and overlooked.

/Be Proud.

The fullness of your features are not a curse.
Your features are to remind you that you are
a divine creation of the creator,
a detailed manifestation of art in human form.
With the passing of every mirror, take a look at yourself,
Look at your eyes,
Look at your nose,
Look at your mouth,
Look at your lips,
Look at your cheekbones,
Look at your complexion,
Take it all in.
It's all intelligently designed.
There were no mistakes made on you.
Your physical make up is a blessing
gifted to anyone who gets to lay eyes on you.
You are a divine experience.

/I See You.

To the girls with big soup coolin' lips..
Lips that reflect ancestral features..
Lips that carry defining attributes..
Lips that were perfectly crafted by the divine herself...
I see you.

/Black Hair Part II.

So often,
thick, course, healthy hair,
is deemed nappy.
And people actually believe it.
Do my curls not define themselves enough for you?
Everybody's hair tells a different story and sings a different tune.
Fuck a hair chart.
Continue to pour love onto your roots,
no matter how thick, or undefinable.
Your hair connects you to something greater.
Black hair is power.
It defies gravity.
It has character.
It holds history.
It does not come in a "one texture fits all" box.

/Magic.

Carry your magic everywhere you go.
Turn everything you touch into gold.
You are valuable.
You don't ever have to compromise who you are
in order to make others more accepting of you.
You were not created to be shaped into
who others think you should be.
You are free to be who you want to be.
You are free to act how you want to act.
You are free to speak how you want to speak.
You are free to wear what you want to wear.
You are free to style your hair in any way
you decide to style your hair.
You are free to carry your magic however you choose.
You are not obligated to force yourself to fit into any box.
You do not have to give any explanation
for knowing your worth and embodying your truth.
Being a black woman does not mean you are limited,
You my darling, are limitless.
Own your entire being.
Present your black girl magic in YOUR way,
unapologetically...

[insert finger snap and neck roll here]

/The Natural State Of Black Hair.

To those who wonder why a black girl
embracing her natural hair is such a big deal...
when you live in a world that rejects
the natural presence of a black woman,
taking a stand to embrace it,
becomes a revolutionary act.
So whenever you see a sistah embracing her afro,
braids, locs, kinks and twists,
It should not come as a shock.
Nor should it be met with eye rolls,
weird stares, or the need to touch.
Stop trying to stuff us into
your little standard box of European beauty.
It does not apply here.

/Image.

Little black girls probably struggle with self-image the most.
Being constantly told by society
what you should and shouldn't look like
in order to be considered beautiful,
is beyond detrimental to our community.
What happens when those same little girls become women?
They often grow into their insecurities instead of out of them,
due to the overwhelming pressure to fit
the mold of beauty created by a white washed society.
The beauty of a black woman goes far beyond
the basics of what's generally accepted.
There is no standard beauty,
we come in all shapes, shades, and sizes.
"Standard" cannot exist within a race of people
who produce so much diversity when it comes to aesthetics.

/Beauty.

The idea of beauty goes beyond being physically quantified.
The concept of being beautiful is a full experience.
Love yourself whole,
from the thickness of your roots to the depths of your soul.
Your self-image is exactly that,
the image of yourself created by you.
No one else should ever be given the power
to manipulate your vision of yourself.
Beauty can only be defined by its beholder.
You are its beholder.

/Women.

We continue to separate ourselves from the sisterhood,
even as we attempt to restore it.
As women, we need to understand
that our differences in beliefs, views, and opinions,
should not prevent us from seeing the [crown] in every woman.
We were all gifted with divine feminine energy,
and understanding how to utilize this energy
will help harness our natural power as women,
and further connect us through sisterhood.
We must be very careful to not marginalize
ourselves or each other as we fight for our liberation,
by doing so,
we become the very thing we are fighting against.

/Sisterhood.

Growing up in the same household
with so many different personalities and opinions,
made me realize that people can have the same experience
and still come out of it with different versions of it.
Out of 8 siblings, five of them are sisters.
My sisters are my bloodline tribe.
They helped me embrace the parts of myself
I once ignored or misunderstood.
Our interactions helped me
better connect with other women too.
I no longer envied the magic that
poured from the souls of those who
also carried divine feminine energy.
I discovered my own.
I became full off the magic
I had been suppressing within myself.
Through this sisterhood bonded through blood,
I am able to applaud, admire, and celebrate
other women without thinking I have to dim my own light,
or like there isn't enough empowerment to go around.
Through our connectedness,
I was able to receive the gift of true sisterhood.

/To My Niece Micah.

Babies are so innocent.
So free.
So curious.
They take love and happiness with them everywhere.
They smile for no reason and at every reason.
They have no ulterior motives or objectives,
They are simply being present in their reality.
We teach the babies,
but so often we forget,
we can learn a lot from them too.

/We Are Perfect.

I think we were all made perfectly
but we exist within a society that constantly
makes us feel inferior, imperfect,
and like we are not enough.
Imperfect people fuel capitalism.
We were born with perfect abundance.
Yet we carry the term "imperfect"
as to make ourselves feel better
about the things we think we lack,
or see as "wrong" about ourselves.
I think the concept we have created around imperfection
stops us from growing,
we start to focus so much
on what we think we lack,
we end up intercepting our natural state of evolution.
When a being is birthed into this world
there's nothing to take away, only things to add.
Life should be a constant evolution of perfection
because we should forever be adding to ourselves
as we experience this world.
This brings knowledge, wisdom, truth,
understanding, openness, and continued perfection.
We are not imperfect beings.
We were created perfectly.
We only become imperfect once we stop
giving ourselves room to grow
and attempt to attain artificial perfection
through things outside of ourselves.

/Spirituality.

Anything dealing with a higher power,
the universe,
nature,
or even our interactions with other beings,
is a spiritual experience.
Spirituality is the feeling that there's something
bigger than ourselves at work.
Being spiritual is connecting with yourself
beyond the ego in order to reach a higher consciousness.
It's the cultivation of your direct connection to a higher source.
It's your personal relationship to God.
It's always been weird to me how the idea of God
is taught as being separate from man.
It makes it hard to take responsibility and ownership
for one's own actions and behaviors.
This also takes away from the importance
of having faith in ourselves.
I operate from the belief that
God dwells within us and all around us.
Good and bad also lies within us
because this too, is a part of the "God experience".
It's all within us.
Every day we are consciously and subconsciously
choosing to serve either our higher or lower selves.
I don't see having faith in myself as an act against God,
I see it as the most powerful form of accepting
the presence of God within myself as truth.

/Acceptance.

So many choose to suffer and struggle
because we are taught that life is full of torment,
and experiencing this,
means you are just experiencing what life is.
Through my own experiences I've learned,
I've often been the cause of my own suffering.
Many philosophers and spiritual teachers
constantly speak of reaching a state of "enlightenment",
or self-awareness.
Many have their own teachings and methods
on how to reach this space.
In my understanding,
the only way to reach this,
is through acceptance.
Accepting that there is no right or wrong way to live your life.
Accepting that you have the ability to control
your response to whatever is happening around you.
Accepting that no matter what or who you follow,
be it Buddha, Muhammad, God,
or whatever it is you choose to believe in,
you have to unlock the higher being within yourself.
We all have the ability to reach this "high" state of evolution,
but first we must stop torturing ourselves
into thinking constant suffering is normal.
This life was given to you to enjoy and find fulfillment.
Bliss is your birthright.
Do not foolishly choose
a life of suffering.

/The buildup.

It's such a process to leave what you were initially taught
in order to embrace what you currently know.
Some days I feel I've mastered and conquered this,
while other days I feel I fail miserably.
But sometimes breaking down
is necessary for a more potent build up.

/Reminders About Worth.

Everyone won't see your worth.
Some people just won't be that into who you are,
or what you have to offer.
Do not let this cause you to doubt your greatness,
or the authenticity of your love.
You won't have to convince those who actually want you.
Just keep it moving.
This isn't a loss,
its divine intervention.
You're being prepared for something
and someone far greater.
Accept the blessing.
This is the universe showing you
that you are worthy of more.

/Soul Mates.

I no longer believe we are only granted
one soulmate per lifetime.
I believe we are granted soulmates for
various seasons of our lives.
Sometimes they show up in friendships,
business partnerships,
or in our intimate relationships.
They are sent
to grow us,
to evolve us,
and to introduce us to the next level of ourselves.

/God.

How could we profess an understanding of a higher power,
believe in a higher being,
and doubt our very own ability within the same breath?
Are we not manifestations of this very energy?
We say we are believers,
but are we really?
The moment we stop believing in ourselves,
is the moment we allow doubt
to set-up shop within our consciousness
and impose on our reality.
It's also the very moment we detach ourselves from the truth
of being a part of something greater.
We will forever find ourselves in torment
until we trust the presence of God within ourselves.

/Freedom.

Freedom is not something you ask for,
it's something you have to take.
You can either stay on the plantation
and remain passive to the fact that you're enslaved,
or wake up,
take your freedom,
and escape.
Too many of us got one foot on the plantation
while the other is on free land,
fearing that If we completely disconnected
from this system of mass oppression,
all hope may be lost.
The biggest accomplishment of this system,
has been its ability to convince us all
that we have little power over our own lives.
It has convinced us that we need it to survive.
It has made us dependent on their false teachings
and dismissive of our own understandings.
It has caused us to hold on for dear life
to the very system that has kept its foot on our necks.

BLOOM.

(the wisdom gained from
a new awareness of self)

/The Light.

Self-awareness can be a struggle at first sight.
Being able to really see yourself,
takes a lot of honesty and acceptance.
There's a possibility you may not like what you see,
but being able to accept this truth,
and being willing to put in the necessary work
it will take to grow into a better version of yourself,
will create a type of awareness that will refuse
to stay hidden in the dark.
It will force you and all that you are
into the light
and you will thrive!

/The Journey.

I am on the journey of evolving into the highest version of myself.
As we all should be.
On this journey,
I have visited the remains
of past states of mind many times.
I have brushed shoulders with memories
I never laid to rest and retreated back
to parts of me I no longer resonate with,
all in the name of comfort.
I have made mistake after mistake along the way.
I have cried.
Been depressed.
I have used people to fill voids only I could fill,
and been disappointed time and time again
when I still encountered holes within my soul.
They couldn't save me.
I constantly searched for myself
through eyes that were not my own.
It wasn't until I faced myself
that I was finally able to reach enlightenment.
Only then was I able to bloom.

/Choose Wisely.

You can either take a role as a victim or victor.
You can spend your days complaining,
or you can spend them healing and growing.
We all must slay our personal demons
when trying to evolve.
This process can be brutal.
You will feel like you are at war with yourself,
and this can be painful,
but the transition you will undergo
will shine light on a type of freedom
you have never experienced.
This is evolution.

/The Experience.

Since I have allowed myself to evolve,
I've been experiencing God,
the intimacy of love,
and I've been able to boldly present
my truths without apology.
For this I am grateful.

/Peace & Blessings.

I finally channeled my inner Goddess
and found the inner peace
I had been searching for most of my life.
I decided to stop letting others shape the way I saw myself.
I decided to stop looking for myself within the world
and started to cultivate the world within myself.
I am no longer afraid to allow love within my space.
I am no longer afraid to let my mind evolve into another galaxy.
I am no longer afraid to let my soul
dance around the brim of the sun,
or sleep in the corners of the moon.
I am the creator of my own universe
and realizing this forced me to see life differently.
When you work on being a more
loving and happier person to yourself,
you will attract more love and happiness into your orbit,
and you will discover peace and prosperity
flowing abundantly within your realm.

/Discovery.

I rediscovered my beauty
while applying my truth to the creases of my soul.
And with this,
I was able to fall deeply in love
with the woman I am.
A woman in love with herself
is a woman every man should try to keep
and the kind of woman
every woman should want to be,
because a woman in love with her own presence
is a magical force.
The universe will always manifest in her honor
and bow to her grace.

/A Moment of Reflection.

Be whatever it is you expect of others.
Reach your own standards first.
You can require a lot
when you have a lot to offer.

/Relationships.

A man is not the blame for you "going crazy".
A man is not the blame for your low self-esteem.
A man can contribute to these things
but a man is not responsible for you choosing
to stay in a space that is unloving to your soul.
We so easily blame men for our own self-destruction.
Love does not make you stay where love is not present.
A lack of love for yourself makes you stay
because anyone who truly love themselves
will not settle for lesser treatment.
Many women have lost their worth
at the hands of a man
simply because they went against themselves.
If you truly see yourself as a Queen,
you will always demand royal treatment,
and a good man will never give you anything less.
We always accept what we think we deserve.
The times I was served mistreatment,
it was my responsibility to remove myself from the table,
no one else's.
I had to learn to take accountability
for the type of people I was attracting into my life
and own up to the role I played
in birthing my own heartbreaks.

/Love Can Be A Waiting Game.

Countless times,
I found myself settling
because I thought what I desired may have been unrealistic.
I thought what I wanted could only be found
within the scripts of romantic comedies
or within the lyrics of 90's R&B love song.
But I've realized,
you can't let a few unfortunate encounters with love
cause you to doubt love's possibilities.
Just because you have yet to experience
the kind of love you desire,
doesn't mean it isn't on its way to you...

/Attraction.

The type of attraction that goes beyond the physical
because you are so fixated on the beauty of their soul.
The type of attraction that pulls you in
before you even realize how deep you actually are.
The type of attraction that words just won't do justice.
The type of attraction that binds beings
into a blissful state of harmony.
The type of attraction that emits
a vibe so powerful,
your spirit orgasms into a new dimension
as you meet yourself through
the heart of someone else.
You deserve this type of attraction
because this type of attraction exists.

/The Relationship Concept.

After experiencing different relationships,
I finally understand what a relationship should be,
at least to me...
Relationships should be seen as partnerships.
You become a team.
You work together to build up the strongest bond possible.
You try to only make decisions
that will uplift and positively benefit the union.
You understand that it is a learning process for all involved.
You challenge each other to be better.
You contribute to the growth of the partnership.
You add to the collaboration.
You make sure your goals and interests are in sync.
You become each other's allies.
The commitment you make to the relationship
becomes your alliance.

/No Love Lost.

I'm learning to never regret giving love to someone
just because they didn't, or wasn't able to give
the same kind of love back.
Sometimes people come into our lives
to receive the love they don't have to give
and sometimes people come to give us
the kind of love we have longed to receive.

/The Reintroduction to Love.

Love didn't come wrapped how I initially imagined.
It wasn't a violent wave crashing up against my shoreline.
It didn't make my heart beat a million miles per hour.
It wasn't this grand public display of fireworks.
I didn't feel like I was losing my mind.
Instead,
love came as a kiss upon my collar bone.
As a gentle breeze across my lips.
It appeared as a rush of calming waves
dancing under the spell of the moon.
Love showed up in my life offering balance.
It didn't make me feel like an addict.
It wasn't extreme.
This kind of love came as a release.
I felt peace, sober, and free.
It was nothing how I thought it was supposed to be
but it was everything I needed.
It made me feel sane again.
It restored my faith in love's details.

/Level Up.

Your journey is yours.
Your dreams are yours.
Don't try to force people into seeing and believing
what the divine created for only your eyes to see,
those needed, will be drawn into your space.
You won't have to chase, beg, or force their love or support.
You will attract who and what's for you,
when it's time to.
Your job is to just stay the course.
Everything is unfolding as it should.
Connect the dots and count your blessings.
The person who learns that there's no greater love
than a love that is birthed from within,
and that success is understanding that you are the creator of it,
will always be the most successful and most loved
person in the room.

/Money Bags.

I knew I had to change the way I viewed money
if I was going to ever break the lack of money cycle
that has circulated throughout my family tree.
I had to stop seeing money as something
that was not important because it is.
Money isn't everything but it's necessary.
It can be hard to develop proper money making principles
when you grow up without it,
but it's the only way to escape
and change that reality.
Poverty is a two-fold experience.
It affects your mind and your pockets.
If you find abundance within your thoughts,
It will be easier to manifest it in your bank account.
You will start making sound investments,
finding financial freedom,
and creating generational wealth.

/Master Self and Know Freedom.

Mastering yourself is the key to your freedom.
It took me a long time to learn how to heal myself,
and I am still learning.
Facing ourselves can be torture.
It's funny how much guilt and regret
you can build up when you are not living your life authentically.
I had to forgive myself.
Sometimes we keep ourselves in the cocoon phase,
neglecting the fact that becoming a butterfly is our fate.
But once you finally trust your own wings,
you fly.

/Forward Movements.

Moving on can be one of the hardest things you ever have to do.
It's hard because memories are forever
embedded within the crevice of our minds.
It's hard because... well... breaking habits and routines
are just generally hard to do.
It's hard because when you are used to something or someone,
it becomes a task exerting energy
to act like the experience never happened.
So how do you move on?
By simply taking a step forward every single day
and by not trying to erase the memories,
but learning to accept what was,
what is,
and what will be.

/Pack Light.

Once you release the things that weigh you down,
the journey becomes lighter.
It's really that simple.

/Get High.

High self-esteem and confidence are two things
every soul should be equipped with,
if we depend on others to feed our self-esteem,
or to supply our confidence,
we will constantly rise and fall
at the hands of those whom we have given this power.
We will forever seek validation outside of ourselves
and this is the worst kind of disease one can be inflicted with.
You are the only person qualified enough
to validate your existence and your space here on this earth.
Never relinquish your power or right to do so.
You are not inferior to anyone.
Think highly of yourself
and act in alignment with that.
When one has a high dose of self- confidence,
they are less likely to become a slave
to the thoughts and beliefs of others.

/Enlightenment.

Self-awareness is one of the most beautiful
forms of enlightenment.
Becoming more aware of myself
helped me to connect more with my emotions,
which was necessary for me to be able
to start the healing process I needed to evolve.
The experiences and lessons I've been given along the way,
have been water and sunlight for my journey.

/I am.

We were all created to
shine,
glow,
and prosper in all that we are.
Without doubt.
Without shame.
Without envy.
We are here to birth our best selves
through the discovery of our highest potential.
We are here to stand full
in our wholeness.
We are here to embrace our perfection
because perfect, we are.
I am.
You are.

/Rise.

I rise for those who have unfairly fallen through
the cracks of the system.
I rise for those who didn't think it was possible.
I rise for those who are too afraid
to trust their own ascension.
I rise to let you know it's possible.
I rise to let you know there's nothing to fear.
I rise because I'm way too fly not to.

/The Message.

There are so many more revelations I have to share
but I wanted this to be subtle.
Truth can be a hard pill to swallow,
so I had to give you a glass of water first.
I wrote this book because I was tired
of holding these words within.
This book symbolizes the shedding of my layers,
the blossoming of awareness,
and the removal of my mask.
The process of blooming
can be a lot of things
but above all else,
It's a beautiful discovery of self.
And it's only the beginning...

To all the
Black Girls Bloomin'...

Bloom baby, bloom.

About The Author

Chandra Meadows is a black girl bloomin'.
She spends her days writing, creating, making mistakes and living.
Join the #BlackGirlBloomin movement
by using the hashtag.

To connect via social media:
IG: @BlackGirlBloomin
BlackGirlBloomin.com

Submit any questions or letters to:
Hello@blackgirlbloomin.com

www.ingramcontent.com/pod-product-compliance
Lightning Source LLC
Chambersburg PA
CBHW071953100426
42736CB00043B/3089